PRAYERS TO GUIDE TEACHING

The Spiritual and Pastoral Texts and Resources Division

Alliance for Catholic Education Press
at the University of Notre Dame

PRAYERS
TO
GUIDE
TEACHING

Gail Mayotte, SASV

ALLIANCE FOR CATHOLIC EDUCATION PRESS
AT THE UNIVERSITY OF NOTRE DAME

NOTRE DAME, INDIANA

Text design by Julie Wernick Dallavis & Gail Mayotte, SASV

Cover and text image by Gertrude Crete, SASV
   "Within the fire of prayer a hand opens in self-gift."

Cover design by Mary Jo Adams Kocovski

Library of Congress Cataloging-in-Publication Data

Mayotte, Gail.
  Prayers to guide teaching / Gail Mayotte.
     p. cm.
  ISBN 978-0-9788793-2-7 (pbk. : alk. paper)
  1. Christian educators--Religious life. 2. Spiritual life--Catholic Church. 3.
Prayer--Catholic Church. I. Title.

  BV4596.E38M39 2007
  268'.7--dc22

                              2007006933

∞ This book was printed on acid-free paper.

Printed in the United States of America

CONTENTS

Introduction   *ix*

The Respectful Teacher   2

To Teach With Understanding   4

The Peaceful Teacher   6

To Teach With Integrity   8

The Generous Teacher   10

To Teach With Hope   12

The Empowering Teacher   14

To Teach With Courage   16

The Listening Teacher   18

To Teach With Vision   20

The Passionate Teacher   22

To Teach With Gentleness   24

The Joyful Teacher   26

To Teach With Wisdom   28

The Caring Teacher   30

To Teach With Patience   32

The Just Teacher   34

To Teach With Gratitude   36

The Resourceful Teacher   38

To Teach With Prudence   40

To all teachers
who seek God's grace
and reveal God's love.

INTRODUCTION

What virtues guide your teaching? How do they inform the decisions you make? How do others experience them through their interactions with you? In a profession that touches lives through effective communication and sound instructional choices, these are important questions to consider. Taking time to pray about the values guiding your teaching and letting God speak to you through scripture and daily experiences provides opportunity to explore the answers and to be open to invitations for growth.

This book consists of a series of prayers related to qualities for teaching. It is by no means complete, but it does provide an invitation to look closely at one's teaching in light of some important values.

The prayers in this book may be prayed individually or communally. As a resource for personal reflection they offer a specific focus to guide one's personal prayer. Some possible ideas for individual use of the prayers:

- Choose one of the values as a personal focus for a given week and use the prayer associated with it as a means to be attentive to the value expressed through one's teaching. Consider beginning each day praying the prayer of the chosen theme. Take time to ponder the reflection question and let it speak to your experiences. You might also consider copying one of the scriptural phrases and placing it in your calendar or on your desk for easy viewing.

- Cycle through the themes of the prayers over the course of a month with each day focusing on a different one. Begin each day praying the prayer of the chosen theme. Take time to ponder the reflection question and let it speak to your experiences. You might consider jotting the theme of the prayer on to your daily calendar as a reminder of your chosen focus for the day.

- Pray one of the prayers and journal your reactions, reflections, experiences and/or insights.

- Revisit a chosen prayer at the end of the day. Let your reflection relive the school day and provide a memory of the theme experienced or acted upon.

- As a night prayer, reflect on the day's events and choose a value that was especially alive and active or absent and needed. Pray for the grace to live the value going forward.

The prayers might also be used in group settings with the reflection questions as a possible impetus for faith sharing. When prayed in a communal setting, the text in bold print is meant to be a choral response. Some possible ideas for communal use of the prayers:

- Open the school day or begin a faculty meeting by sharing one of the prayers.

- Choose a small segment from one of the prayers (a sentence or stanza) and use it for a shared faculty prayer.

- Choose one of the qualities as a monthly school focus and use the prayer to facilitate a faith sharing with faculty members during a scheduled faculty meeting. Throughout the month, post one of the scriptural references in the faculty lounge as a reminder of the shared focus.

- Give out one of the prayers to faculty members a week prior to a meeting. Invite teachers to reflect upon their experiences of the value throughout the week. Invite sharing on those recognitions during the meeting.

- Gather a small group of teacher colleagues for weekly prayer and faith sharing. Choose a different theme for each week.

- Choose a prayer to begin a meeting that responds to a current need within the school. Allow the prayer and sharing to generate healing, awareness, or whatever grace is needed.

- Choose one of the qualities as a retreat day focus and provide time for both personal and communal prayer related to the theme.

In whatever way you choose to use these prayers, as you undertake them, may you be blessed with an open mind and willing heart to receive God's graces and to truly be the teacher God is calling forth.

THE PRAYERS

# The Respectful Teacher

Give honor to all, love the community, fear God, honor the king. (I Peter 2:17)

I pray, loving God,
that you keep me mindful
of my responsibility and desire
to share through my teaching
the utmost respect
in word, in action, in thought
and in prayer.

With Jesus as my model,
May I choose humble actions,
gentle listening, wise words
and an honoring presence.

If I am less than respectful,
I pray for forgiveness.
If I am curt or arrogant,
I pray for awareness.
If I am preoccupied or distant,
I pray for attention.

Loving God,
help me to treat each person
with the same level of respect.
Help me to reveal to my
students that I value their
presence and their being.
Shape my words and actions
to reveal your gentle kindness.
Mark my teaching with
humility and reverence
for others.

Through these actions, may
others know the sincerity of
encouraging phrases, trusting
looks, and valued presence.

For this I pray. Amen.

SUGGESTED READING:
   John 4:4-30

Reflection: Recall an event
from past experiences or
choose a passage from this
prayer and reflect on how it
calls you to be a respectful
teacher and colleague.

PRAYERS OF PETITION:

**Response: Only with
respect will I grow in the
Lord.**

May I give respect,
understanding and presence to
those I teach.

May I respect the variety of
gifts in my classroom.

May I show respect for the gifts
God has given me.

May respect fill my thoughts
and actions.

CLOSING: Loving God, teach
me gentleness and respect and
guide my words and actions. To
be a respectful teacher, I need
your guidance. For this I pray.
Amen.

To Teach With Understanding

Who among you is wise and understanding? Let this show by good behavior and deeds in the gentleness of wisdom. (James 3:13—adapted)

Loving God,
Fill me this day with the
understanding of mind
to be fully awake to your
presence in my classroom.

Help me to accept that teaching
is a learning process—a never
ending exposure to new ideas,
best practices, and novel
approaches.
The art of teaching is learned
little by little;
the skill of teaching is practiced
moment by moment.

Bless me with openness this
day that I might learn through
my responsibilities.
Bless me with awareness that I
might perceive pressing needs.
Bless me with recognition that
I might act with wisdom and
understanding.

**By wisdom a house is built,
And by understanding it is
established.
(Proverbs 24:3)**

Loving God,
Fill me this day with the
understanding of heart
to be fully alive to your
presence in my students.

Help me to believe that to
touch others through my
teaching is a learning process—
a never ending commitment to
kind words, patient responses,
and tender support.
The skill of touching others is
learned little by little;
the act of touching others is
practiced moment by moment.

Bless me with gratitude this
day that I might appreciate the
individuality of each student I
teach.
Bless me with insight that I
might read struggles and find
the right words to comfort.
Bless me with intuition that I
might recognize unstated needs
and respond in loving ways.

**By wisdom a house is built,
And by understanding it is
established.**

Loving God,
Fill me this day with
understanding of mind and
heart to be fully present in all I
undertake. For this I pray.
Amen.

SUGGESTED READING:
1 John 5:20

Reflection: Recall an event
from your past experiences or
choose a passage from this
prayer and reflect on how it
calls you to be an understanding
teacher.

PRAYERS OF PETITION

**Response: May you be
filled with the "knowledge
of His will in all spiritual
wisdom and understanding."
(Colossians 1:9)**

For understanding of mind and
heart to better embrace the
responsibility of my position.

For understanding of mind and
heart to better comprehend
God's revelation revealed daily
through my teaching.

For understanding of mind and
heart to better respond with
wise words and well-chosen
actions.

CLOSING: To be an
understanding teacher I need
your guidance. For this I pray.
Amen.

The Peaceful Teacher

Grace and peace be multiplied to you in the knowledge of God and of Jesus our Lord. (2 Peter 1:2)

In the serene stillness of the early morning,
    within the walls of my tranquil lodging,
    before the clamor of activity,
    as I enjoy this quiet moment,
    I drink in your peace, O Lord.

And the peace of God, which surpasses all comprehension, will guard your hearts and your minds in Christ Jesus. (Philippians 4:7)

In the chaotic bustle of the hectic school day,
    within the walls of my lively classroom,
    before the ringing of the final bell,
    as I enjoy this dynamic moment,
    I carry your peace, O Lord.

And the peace of God, which surpasses all comprehension, will guard your hearts and your minds in Christ Jesus.

In the informal exchanges of
the after school hours,
   within the walls of my
   emptying building, but
   before the movement to
   homes and families,
   as I enjoy this social
   moment,
   I share your peace, O Lord.

And the peace of God, which surpasses all comprehension, will guard your hearts and your minds in Christ Jesus.

In the waning moments of
enveloping darkness,
   within the walls of my
   silent being,
   before the hush of evening
   falls,
   as I enjoy this silent
   moment,
   I savor your peace, O Lord.

SUGGESTED READING:
   Colossians 3:14-17

Reflection: Recall an event from past experiences or choose a passage from this prayer and reflect on how it calls you to be a peaceful teacher and colleague.

PRAYERS OF PETITION:

Response: May the Lord of peace Himself continually grant you peace in every circumstance. (2 Thessalonians 3:16)

May peace be in my words that I reveal God's tenderness through all I say.

May peace be in my actions that I show God's gentleness in all I do.

May peace be in my thoughts that I ponder God's goodness in all I contemplate.

CLOSING: Loving God, continually grant me peace in every circumstance. To be a peaceful teacher I need your guidance. For this I pray. Amen.

To Teach With Integrity

For my integrity you have supported me and let me stand in your presence forever. (Psalm 41:13)

Sound judgment, and ethical decision making,
In my integrity you uphold me.

Sincere words and honorable actions,
In my integrity you uphold me.

Moral living and upright deeds,
In my integrity you uphold me.

Honest dealings and truthful encounters,
In my integrity you uphold me.

Genuine acts of goodness and authentic presence,
In my integrity you uphold me.

Simple authority and bold veracity,
In my integrity you uphold me.

Generous God,
when day is done
and my body longs for rest
may sleep come easily
to an upright spirit.
For this I pray. Amen.

SUGGESTED READING:
  Matthew 22: 15-22

Reflection: Recall an event from your past experiences or choose a passage from this prayer and reflect on how it calls you to be a person of integrity. How does this impact your teaching?

PRAYERS OF PETITION:

**Response: Let honesty and virtue preserve me; I wait for you, O Lord.
(Psalm 25:21)**

May I make sound judgments and ethical decisions in all I undertake.

May I speak sincere words and be honorable in all my actions.

May I live morally and display upright deeds.

May my dealings with others be honest and may my encounters be truthful.

May I commit genuine acts of goodness and be an authentic presence to those I meet.

May my teaching speak with simple authority and bold veracity.

CLOSING: Generous God, to be a person of integrity and an upright teacher I need your guidance. For this I pray. Amen.

The Generous Teacher

Give freely and not with ill will; for the Lord, your God, will bless you for this in all your works and undertakings. (Deuteronomy 15:10)

The generous teacher gives from the heart and attends to the needs of all students.
The generous teacher helps others.

Give generously "for the Lord, your God, will bless you for this in all your works and undertakings." (Deuteronomy 15:10)

The generous teacher gives confidence and provides ongoing encouragement.
The generous teacher supports others.

Give generously "for the Lord, your God, will bless you for this in all your works and undertakings."

The generous teacher gives with joy and rejoices in all student successes.
The generous teacher celebrates others.

Give generously "for the Lord, your God, will bless you for this in all your works and undertakings."

The generous teacher gives opportunity and invites students to share their gifts.
The generous teacher enables others.

Give generously "for the Lord, your God, will bless you for this in all your works and undertakings."

The generous teacher gives thanks to God and knows all gifts are meant to be shared.
The generous teacher serves others.

Give generously "for the Lord, your God, will bless you for this in all your works and undertakings."

SUGGESTED READING:
  2 Corinthians 9:6-8

Reflection: Recall an event from past experiences or choose a passage from this prayer and reflect on how it calls you to be a generous teacher and colleague.

PRAYERS OF PETITION:

Response: What you have received freely from God give freely to others.

I have been given talents and qualities that transfer to teaching *(pause to name)*

I have been given messages of hope that sustain my teaching *(pause to name)*

I have been given meaningful relationships that support me in my teaching *(pause to name)*

I have been given opportunities to learn that strengthen my teaching *(pause to name)*

CLOSING: Generous God, to be a generous teacher I need your guidance. For this I pray.
Amen.

To Teach With Hope

For I know well the plans I have in mind for you, plans to give you a future full of hope. (Jeremiah 29:11)

God of my hope, in and
through my teaching,

I occasionally hear the
   discouragement in recounts
   of failed attempts
   and see the despair that can
   lead a child to inertia.
I occasionally taste the doubt
   of my own abilities
   and feel the pressure of my
   immense responsibilities.

But I am not paralyzed and I
am not discouraged.
You give me strength and you
give me hope.

**O God, I place all my hope
in you.**

God of my hope, in and
through my teaching,

I occasionally hear the
   exclamations of success
   and witness the spirit that
   won't succumb to adversity.
I occasionally taste the
   assurance that comes with
   affirmation and feel the
   power of trust others have
   in me.

I am encouraged and I am
energized,
You give me joy and you give
me hope.

**O God, I place all my hope
in you.**

God of my hope, in and through my teaching,

I desire to bring hope;
  to speak words of
  encouragement
  and reveal positive energy.
I desire to be hopeful;
  to remain optimistic
  and move forward with
  confidence.
I am your instrument and I
am your servant.
You give me purpose and you
give me hope.

O God, I place all my hope in you.

SUGGESTED READING:
  Romans 5:1-5

Reflection: Recall an event or choose a passage from this prayer and reflect on how it calls you to be a person of hope. How does this inform your teaching?

PRAYER OF PETITION

**Response: May the God of hope fill you with all joy, so that you may abound in hope by the power of the Holy Spirit.
(Romans 15:13)**

God of my hope, in and through me, be the hope that (*choose one of the following and pray for the grace to sustain your desire*)

  speaks words of
  encouragement.

  reveals positive energy.

  remains optimistic.

  moves forward with
  confidence.

CLOSING: God of hope, to teach with hope I need your guidance. For this I pray. Amen.

The Empowering Teacher

It is God who arms me with strength and makes my way perfect. He makes my feet like the feet of a deer; he enables me to stand on the heights.(Psalm 18:32-34)

Source of my strength,
   In weakness I have been carried,
   when insecure I have been encouraged;
   at moments of wanting to give up
   I have been whispered calming words of belief and support.

You are the source of my strength, loving God.
When I need to stand on the heights, you provide me with feet like a deer.

Help me to be a source of strength for my students and to support them with steady encouragement.

Source of my courage,
   In worry I have been lifted,
   when fearful I have been challenged;
   in moments of cowardice
   I have been spoken daring words of confidence and trust.

You are the source of my courage, loving God.
When I need to soar above my worries, you provide me with wings like an eagle.

Help me be a source of courage for my students and to enable them to have wings of confidence.

Source of my trust,
In doubt I have been
assured,
when frazzled I have been
quieted;
in moments of despair
I have been given tranquil
words of hope and belief.

You are the source of my
trust, loving God.
When I need to believe, you
provide me with trust like a
lamb.

**Help me to be a source of
trust for my students and
to project belief in their
awesome potential.**

SUGGESTED READING:
Mt 16: 18–19

Reflection: Recall an event
from your past experiences or
choose a passage from this
prayer and reflect on how it
calls you to be an empowering
teacher and colleague.

PRAYERS OF PETITION:

**Response: May I empower
others through my
teaching.**

By recognizing the potential in
my students.

By supporting my students in
their growth.

By calling forth the gifts in
my students.

By acknowledging the strengths
in my students.

CLOSING: Loving God, help me
to know that believing in others
and supporting their growth
gives them feet like a deer;
helps to enable them to stand
on the heights. For this I pray.
Amen.

To Teach With Courage

Be strong and courageous. Do not be afraid or tremble at them, for the LORD your God is the one who goes with you. He will not fail you or forsake you. (Deuteronomy 31:6)

I need courage.
Every day I am called upon to
guide student progress,
    to make decisions and solve
    problems,
    to listen to questions and
    speak to myriad matters,
    to teach.

The planning, the grading, the
disciplining,
call for the best that I can give.

**Be strong and let your
heart take courage, all you
who hope in the Lord.
(Psalm 31:24)**

I need courage.
Every day I am called upon to
instruct individuals,
    to motivate the
    unmotivated and challenge
    the curious,
    to deal with the disruptive
    and calm the anxious,
    to relate.

The inquisitive, the
uninterested, the struggling,
call for a personalized
approach to the best
that I can give.

**Be strong and let your
heart take courage, all
you who hope in the Lord.**

I need courage.
Every day, I need your help,
Loving God,
    to make wise decisions and
    feel confident in my choices
    to work for what is right and
    possess the strength
    to act.
With your grace, power and
spirit, call forth the best that I
can give.

**Be strong and let your
heart take courage, all you
who hope in the Lord.**

SUGGESTED READING:
    Mt 14:22-33

Reflection: Recall an event
from past experiences or
choose a passage from this
prayer and reflect on how it
calls you to have courage. How
does this impact your teaching?

PRAYERS OF PETITION:

**Response: Stand firm in
faith; be a person of
courage; be strong.**

When tackling difficult
decisions may I...

When fearing going forward
may I...

When doubting my abilities
may I...

When facing challenges to my
convictions may I...

CLOSING: To be a courageous
teacher I need your guidance.
For this I pray. Amen.

The Listening Teacher

Make me know your ways, O LORD; teach me your paths. Lead me in your truth and teach me, for you are the God of my salvation; For you I wait all the day. (Psalm 25:4-5)

Listening God, give ear to my voice and hear the sincerity of my prayer.
What I desire is to listen
 not with the ears of responsibility that must act upon spoken words,
 not with the ears of vulnerability that must face my own insecurities,
 not with the ears of culpability that must account for interpreted actions.
But to listen with the ears of sensitivity, tenderness and compassion so that uttered words are reverenced, connections are felt and responses are spoken with love.

Guide me in your truths, Listening God, and teach me the fine art of listening.

Teach me, O God, to listen
with care and to listen fully
as Your Son did with those he
encountered.
 To the Samaritan woman he
 spoke truths in gentleness.
 To the woman at the feast
 he let her words touch his
 compassion.
 To the children he tenderly
 called, "let them come."
Acknowledging the other
 with presence and focus,
 with peace and gentleness
 of spirit,
 with honesty and openness;
 these are touches of light I
 know through your Son.
May I embrace them in my
moments of listening to others.

**Guide me in your truths,
Listening God, and teach
me the fine art of listening.**

Opportunities abound each day
for sharing and for
communicating, for making
connections and for building
relationships.
 May I pause in my busy days
 to take the time to listen well.
 May I probe with gentle and
 kind words the depth of
 meaning in what another is
 saying.
In my encounters help me
desire to hear other that they
may feel your loving touch.

**Guide me in your truths,
Listening God, and teach
me the fine art of listening.**

SUGGESTED READING:
 Luke 24:13-35

Reflection: Recall an event
from your past experiences or
choose a passage from this
prayer and reflect on how it
calls you to be a listening
teacher and colleague.

PRAYERS OF PETITION:

**Response: Guide me in
your truths, Listening God,
and teach me the fine art of
listening.**

May I hear the calls of those
who suffer because they are not
listened to.

May my listening build
relationships.

May my encounters be
meaningful exchanges.

May I listen to self with the
same care and concern as I do
with others.

CLOSING: Listening God, help
me know the contradiction that
the gentler the listening the
more powerful it becomes. To
be a listening teacher I need
your guidance. For this I pray.
Amen.

To Teach With Vision

Without vision, the people perish.
(Proverbs 29:18 adapted)

Through the school day
labyrinth you make your way
and guide others.
With every few steps decisions
are required that will impact
those following your lead.
Settle for sameness when
something more is demanded
and you reach a dead end.
Choose innovation when
change isn't needed and you
face a wall of darkness.

The right path is before you
leading to potential and
possibility.
Will you make the right choice?

With visionary teachers as your
models
look to the past for inspiration
and guidance.
With Grace as your guide
look inward for strength and
courage.

Deep within hear a whisper urging you onward:

Never cease to trust, to dream, to create

Never succumb to paralysis when feeling powerless

Never be crushed by the weight of mistakes

Never give up in the face of setbacks

Never settle for less than the best you can give.

Armed with wisdom in one hand and hope in the other choose to move forward.

SUGGESTED READING:
1 Kings 3: 5-12

Reflection: Recall an event from past experiences or choose a passage from this prayer and reflect on how it calls you to teach with vision.

PRAYERS OF PETITION:

Response: Show me the path to life, the fullness of joy in your presence. (Ps 16:11 adapted)

Creator God, nurture the dreams within me that I might inspire those I teach.

Stoke the glowing embers of enthusiasm that I might burn with the passion that I need to make a difference.

Spark the light of truth that I might speak to the inner potential of those with whom I work.

Creator God, be my source of inspiration that I might trust your words and my intuition.

CLOSING: Loving God, show me the path to fullness of life. To teach with vision I need your guidance. For this I pray. Amen.

The Passionate Teacher

Never be lacking in zeal, but keep your spiritual fervor, serving the Lord. (Romans 12:11)

Creator and Sustainer of Life,
You call me to attend to the
Spirit's fire burning deep
within me.
You beckon me to trust in my
dreams and embrace the
challenges they reveal.
You challenge me to act on
what I believe and to do so
with passion, fervor, and
zeal.
I ask you now for courage and
fortitude to sustain my
convictions and commitment.
The daily adventures of
teaching provide me exciting
opportunities to embrace
challenges.
There is no room for
hesitancy or uncertainty.
There is no space for
indecision or doubt.

**Never be lacking in zeal,
but keep your spiritual
fervor, serving the Lord.**

You call me to service
through teaching.
You beckon me to make a
difference in the lives of my
students.
You challenge me to trust in
my skills and abilities.
I ask you now for wisdom
and guidance to sustain my
energy and efforts.
The daily activities of
teaching provide me genuine
opportunities to meet needs.
There is no room for lack of
effort or excuses.
There is no space for
insecurity or complacency.

**Never be lacking in zeal,
but keep your spiritual
fervor, serving the Lord.**

You call me to carry hope in
  my heart.
You beckon me to create
  possibilities when problems
  present themselves.
You challenge me to share of
  my abundance in all I do.
I ask you now for strength and
  stamina to sustain my
  determination and desire.
The daily actions of
  teaching provide me
  authentic opportunities
  to help others.
There is no room for
  apathy or inattention.
There is no space for
  uncaring or indifference.

**Never be lacking in zeal,
but keep your spiritual
fervor, serving the Lord.**

Everyday I pour myself into this
  ministry and I believe in your
  power, O God, to work through
  me.
I trust that the dreams you have
  placed in my heart hold
  promise and I am compelled to
  move onward.
I ask you now for your Grace to
  sustain me. Amen.

SUGGESTED READING:
  Matthew 4: 18-22

Reflection: Recall an event
from past experiences or
choose a passage from this
prayer and reflect on how it
calls you to teach with passion.

PRAYERS OF PETITION:

**Response: Be zealous for
the honor of God.**

For courage and fortitude to
sustain my convictions and
commitment that I may be
zealous for the honor of God.

For the wisdom and guidance
to sustain my energy and
efforts that I may be zealous for
the honor of God.

For strength and stamina to
sustain my determination and
desire that I may be zealous for
the honor of God.

CLOSING: Loving God, to teach
with passion I need your
guidance. For this I pray.
Amen.

To Teach With Gentleness

Walk in a manner worthy of the calling with which you have been called, with all humility and gentleness, with patience, showing tolerance or one another in love, being diligent to preserve the unity of the Spirit in the bond of peace. (Ephesians 4:1-3)

Loving God, I bring before you all of my students and ask that you be with them this day.

The one who will arrive early and the one who will be tardy
The one who will come to school with extra snacks and the one who will come to school hungry
The one whose homework will be neat and complete and the one whose homework has been forgotten.

May I embody Christ's gentle presence as I greet each of my students.

The one who will feel ill and the one who will feel homesick
The one who exudes self-confidence and the one who lacks self-esteem
The one who craves an audience and bullies and the one who craves acceptance and is bullied.

May I embody Christ's gentle presence as I care for each of my students.

The one who never stops
  talking
  and the one who never talks
The one who is very focused
  and the one who is easily
  distracted
The one who never stops
  working and the one who
  never stops moving

May I embody Christ's gentle presence as I attend to each of my students.

The one who will finish all
  work too quickly and the
  one who will not finish any
  work
The one who will find some
  way to correct me and the
  one who will cry when I try
  to make a correction
The one who will use words
  others won't understand
  and
The one who will struggle
  to read this prayer

May I embody Christ's gentle presence as I teach each of my students.

SUGGESTED READING:
  Matthew 11:28-30

Reflection: Recall an event or choose a passage from this prayer and reflect on how it calls you to teach with gentleness.

PRAYERS OF PETITION

Response: Walk in a manner worthy of the calling with which you have been called.

May I embody Christ's gentle presence as I greet each of my students.

May I embody Christ's gentle presence as I care for each of my students.

May I embody Christ's gentle presence as I attend to each of my students.

May I embody Christ's gentle presence as I teach each of my students.

CLOSING: Loving God, to teach with gentleness I need your guidance. For this I pray. Amen.

The Joyful Teacher

But as for me, I shall sing of Your strength; Yes, I shall joyfully sing of Your loving kindness in the morning, for You have been my stronghold and a refuge in the day of my distress. (Psalm 59:16)

Loving Creator,

fill me with a joyful heart
to rejoice in the sacred
and the simple marvels
of this day.

bless me with a deep
sense of wonder to
delight in the mysteries
revealed all around me.

give me a profound sense of
deep gratitude to celebrate
my call to teach and
commitment to serve.

**My mouth offers praises
with joyful lips.
(Psalm 63:5)**

Open to your graces I desire to
sing of your goodness.

Whether I meet with
   resistance or receive
   gestures of approval
Whether I face defiance or
   experience cooperation
Whether I deal with mischief
   or take pleasure in student
   humor
Help me to share joy this day.

My mouth offers praises with joyful lips.

Whether I am rushing to meet
  deadlines or enjoying
  leisure time.
Whether I am resolving peer
  conflict or complimenting
  good deeds
Whether I am feeling near
  exhaustion or brimming
  with newfound energy
Help me to share joy this day.

SUGGESTED READING:
  2 Corinthians 9:6-8

Reflection: Recall an event or
choose a passage from this
prayer and reflect on how it
calls you to be a joyful teacher
and colleague.

PRAYERS OF PETITION

**Response: Be joyful for "a
cheerful heart has a
continual feast."
(Proverbs 15:15)**

Open my eyes, loving Creator,
that I might see the true
marvels of this day
and...

Open my hands, loving Creator,
that I might receive the
wondrous mysteries that are
given to me this day and...

Open my heart, loving Creator
that I might share the deep
gratitude I have for the life and
mission given to me and...

CLOSING: Loving Creator,
fill me with a joyful heart to
rejoice in the sacred and the
simple marvels of this day.

Bless me with a deep sense of
wonder to delight in the
mysteries revealed all around
me.

Give me a profound sense of
deep gratitude to celebrate my
call to teach and commitment
to serve.

To be a joyful teacher I need
your guidance. For this I pray.
Amen.

To Teach With Wisdom

The wisdom from above is first pure, then peaceable, gentle, reasonable, full of mercy and good fruits, unwavering, without hypocrisy. (James 3:17)

The past is rich in storied
wisdom
Lives given to service,
    filled with profound faith
    and passion, open to
    God's transforming grace.
Yesteryears hold the secrets
    of inner strength revealed,
    deep convictions sustained,
    and noble deeds realized.

We desire to work in
    communion with our
    educational ancestors, the
    countless men and women
    who built, staffed, and
    shaped our early schools.

We yearn to know the
    hearts and minds of these
    prophetic treasures who were
    the dreamers and the
    visionaries, the leaders and
    the decision makers, the
    truth seekers and the
    teachers.

We value their commitment
    and beliefs
    and seek their revelations
    and wisdom.

For each one is a blessing.
Each one is a link in the
wisdom story.

Behold, You desire truth in the innermost being, and in the hidden part You will make me know wisdom. (Psalm 51:6)

The future is rich in expectant wisdom
Lives given to opportunity,
    filled with potential and
    promise,
    open to God's transforming
    grace.
Each day holds the mysteries
    of life unfolding, growth
    occurring, opportunity
    beckoning.

We desire to nurture tender
    possibilities, in the
    countless boys and girls
    who attend our schools.

We touch the hearts and
minds of those young treasures
who are destined to become the
dreamers and the visionaries,
the leaders and the decision
makers, the truth seekers and
the teachers.

We value their openness and
    eagerness and seek their
    revelations and truths.

For each one is a blessing.
Each one is a link in the
wisdom story.

Behold, You desire truth in the innermost being, and in the hidden part You will make me know wisdom.

SUGGESTED READING:
    1 Kings 3:5-12

Reflection: Recall an event or choose a passage from this prayer and reflect on how it calls you to teach with wisdom.

PRAYERS OF PETITION

Response: My mouth will speak wisdom, and the meditation of my heart will be understanding. (Psalm 49:3)

Source of Wisdom, help us to take inspired steps as we continue the educational story started by our ancestors.

Source of Wisdom, help us to make wise decisions as we engage in our daily ministry as teachers.

CLOSING: Source of All Knowing, to be a wise teacher I need your guidance. For this I pray. Amen.

The Caring Teacher

Above all, keep fervent in your love for one another, because love covers a multitude of sins. (1 Peter 4:8)

When confusion baffles
  and uncertainty questions
be patient.

When intimidation attacks
  and ignorance insults
be kind.

When defiance erupts
  and non-compliance
  challenges
be respectful.

When needs emerge
  and concerns plead
be generous.

When apathy clouds
  and conformity controls
be compassionate.

When self-defeat chatters
  and effort stumbles
be gentle.

When good will falters
  and mistakes arise
be forgiving.

When success smiles
  and mastery triumphs
be humble.

Loving God,
in all I do this day
help me to touch others
with kind words, loving
actions, gentle concern
and tender care.

May others realize your
goodness acting through me.

For this I pray. Amen.

SUGGESTED READING:
  1 Corinthians 13:1-7

Reflection: Recall an event
from past experiences or
choose a passage from this
prayer and reflect on how it
calls you to be a caring teacher
and colleague.

PRAYER OF PETITION:

Choose the quality of
love—*patience, kindness,
respect, generosity,
compassion, gentleness,
forgiveness, humility*—you
most want to embrace this
day as you reflect care and
concern in your teaching.

Ask God for the grace to
sustain your desire and to
bless your concrete
expressions this day.

CLOSING: Loving God, to be a
caring teacher I need your
guidance. For this I pray.
Amen.

To Teach With Patience

So as those who have been chosen by God, holy and beloved, put on a heart of compassion, kindness, humility, gentleness and patience. (Colossians 3:12)

Loving God, source of all
good things, hear my prayer.

Help me to know patience as
a close friend.
When unforeseen problems
kick up dust and inevitable
challenges stare me in the
face, may patience provide
strength for my teaching.

Help me to know patience as
a wise sage.
When tough decisions
demand insight and difficult
actions need focus and
attention, may patience
companion me in my
teaching.

Help me to know patience as
a soothing balm.
When hectic activity fills my
moments and the day unfolds
at a frenzied pace,
may patience ease pressures
in my teaching.

Loving God, source of all
good things,
Help me to trust the message
of my close friend, Patience:
*"Plan for the unexpected.
Anticipate and overcome
difficulties. Persevere my
friend, persevere."*

Help me to trust the advice of
my wise sage, Patience:

*"Take time to reason well.
Concentrate on the essential
Persist my protégé, persist."*

Help me to feel the comfort of
my soothing balm, Patience:
*"Let go of unnecessary worry
Realize growth over time.
Peace, my enduring one,
peace."*

SUGGESTED READING:
   Romans 15:5-6

Reflection: Recall an event
from past experiences or
choose a passage from this
prayer and reflect on how it
calls you to patience. How does
this impact your teaching?

PRAYERS OF PETITION:

**Response: Clothe me in
patience, loving God.**

When I am engrossed with
urgent needs,

When I am preoccupied with
grave concerns,

When I am frazzled in frantic
rushing,

CLOSING: Loving God, help me
to know patience as a close
friend, wise sage, and soothing
balm. To be a patient teacher I
need your guidance. For this I
pray. Amen.

 # The Just Teacher

And what does the Lord require of you but to do justice, to love kindness, and to walk humbly with your God. (Micah 6:8)

Live with integrity,
  speak with sincerity
Be honest, fair and kind
Turn to Wisdom to guide
decisions
**Seek justice for justice is
with the Lord.**

Respect every individual,
  treat all with dignity
Be supportive and open-
minded
Foster cooperation and
collaboration
**Practice justice for justice
is with the Lord.**

Build community,
  resolve conflicts peacefully,
Be tolerant and flexible
Accentuate peace in all
interactions
**Do justice for justice is
with the Lord.**

Combat prejudice,
  fight discrimination
Be open, alert and aware
Encourage respect for
diversity
**Seek justice for justice is
with the Lord.**

Support the needy,
  help the oppressed
Be strong, committed, and
fervent
Speak for those lacking a voice
**Practice justice for
justice is with the Lord.**

Fight injustice,
  uphold righteousness
Be moral, just, and upright
Work for God's anawim
**Do justice for justice is
with the Lord.**

SUGGESTED READING:
  Mt 12: 16-21

Reflection: Recall an event
from past experiences or
choose a passage from this
prayer and reflect on how it
calls you to be a just teacher.

PRAYERS OF PETITION:

**Response: To do
righteousness and justice is
desired by the Lord**

God of Justice, help us to work
for justice in our schools and in
our world.

Help us to build community
and unite others for the
common good.

Help us to be peacemakers in
all our interactions.

Help us to be a voice against
injustices and inequalities.

CLOSING: Loving God, to be a
just teacher I need your
guidance. For this I pray.
Amen.

To Teach With Gratitude

Devote yourselves to prayer, being watchful and thankful. (Colossians 4:2)

Loving God,
May your presence be felt by
    all who walk through our
    school doors this day.
Help all who pass over their
    thresholds to see you
    in the smiles of students, the
    dedication of teachers, the
    good will of parents, the
    leadership of our principal.
Give all who work behind these
    doors the gifts of patient
    resolve, audacious hope,
    clear vision, and creative
    energy.
Fill all with gratitude for what
    has been and what will be
    through these doors.

Our school doors open to a rich
heritage!
Within them,
    we sense your presence in the
    spirit of founding members
    who continue to whisper their
    influence.
Within them,
    we feel your grace in the
    memory of beloved teachers
    who once spoke your name
    with the same zeal it is voiced
    today.
Within them,
    we know your glory in the
    timeless pictures and
    symbols that adorn the walls.

These reminders of years past strengthen our commitment to teaching today and we are grateful.

Our school doors open to a community of faith!
Through them,
 we sense your presence in the community that expresses its faith in word and action.
Through them,
 we feel your grace in the service that reaches out to many.
Through them,
 we know your glory in the values and Gospel message woven into daily lessons.
These touches of light strengthen our beliefs and give us hope for the future. And we are grateful.

Loving God,
Fill us with a grateful heart for what has been and what will be revealed through these doors this day. We pray this in the name of Jesus. Amen.

SUGGESTED READING:
 Colossians 3:14-17

Reflection: Recall an event from past experiences or choose a passage from this prayer and reflect on how it calls you to gratitude. How does this impact your teaching?

PRAYERS OF PETITION:

Response: Give thanks to the Lord, for he is good; his love endures forever. (1 Chronicles 16:34)

For our school founder and the people and events that have shaped our school in a significant way throughout its history *(pause to name)...*

For our school community of faith and the people and events that give life to our current identity *(pause to name)...*

CLOSING: To teach with gratitude I need to be mindful of our school's history, community, purpose, and people. To teach with gratitude I need your guidance. For this I pray. Amen

The Resourceful Teacher

Now finish the work, so that your eager willingness to do it may be matched by your completion of it, according to your means. For if the willingness is there, the gift is acceptable according to what one has, not according to what he does not have. (2 Corinthians 8:11-12)

It would be helpful to have the latest technology to bring the world of virtual learning into my classroom.

It would be beneficial to have the newest textbooks so that images and information are up-to-date.

It would be valuable to have access to art supplies, graphing calculators, or even paper so that basic materials are available to my students.

I could lament what I don't have or I can acknowledge what I possess, a willing heart, ingenuity, and initiative.

I ask you loving God to bless these resources that my students' lives will be touched in positive ways and learning can occur.

It would be helpful to have classroom renovations to provide more conveniences for learning.

It would be beneficial to take extra field trips to introduce my students to novel experiences beyond the classroom.

It would be valuable to have access to services and extra support staff to address needs beyond the academic.

I could complain about what I don't have or I can appreciate what I possess, a cooperative spirit, imagination and inspiration.

I ask you loving God to bless these resources that my students' lives will be touched in positive ways and learning can occur.

It would be helpful to have access to more supplementary materials and resources to enrich my teaching.

It would be beneficial to have more time for planning and preparing lessons.

It would be valuable to have unlimited financial resources to

afford more opportunities for professional development.

I could bemoan what I don't have or I can work with what I possess, diligence, resourcefulness, and an indomitable spirit.

I ask you loving God to bless these resources that my students' lives will be touched in positive ways and learning can occur.

SUGGESTED READING:
   Matthew 25:14-30

Reflection: Recall an event or choose a passage from this prayer and reflect on how it calls you to be a resourceful teacher.

PRAYER OF PETITION

Take time to name the resources with which God has blessed you. Ask God for the grace to use them well for the good of others.

CLOSING: Loving God, thank you for my gifts and for the chance to work within my school. Bless me and the resources I bring. To be a resourceful teacher I need your guidance. For this I pray. Amen.

To Teach With Prudence

I, wisdom, dwell with prudence, and I find knowledge and discretion. (Proverbs 8:12)

The mind of the prudent
acquires knowledge, and
the ear of the wise seeks
knowledge.
(Proverbs 18:15)

When difficult decisions need
to be made
The mind of the prudent
acquires knowledge.

And seeking advice will
inform options
The ear of the wise seeks
knowledge.

When intricate matters
demand sound judgment
The mind of the prudent
acquires knowledge.

And guidance will enlighten
all choices
The ear of the wise seeks
knowledge.

When potential problems
benefit from foresight
The mind of the prudent
acquires knowledge.

And important information
can be learned from others
The ear of the wise seeks
knowledge.

When realizing responsibility
to be prepared
The mind of the prudent
acquires knowledge.

And capable others are all
around
The mind of the prudent
acquires knowledge.

SUGGESTED READING:
  Matthew 25:1-13

Reflection: Recall an event or
choose a passage from this
prayer and reflect on how it
calls you to teach with
prudence.

PRAYERS OF PETITION

Response: The prudent
act with knowledge.

For the gift of discretion that
I might use good judgment
about what should and
should not be said.

For the gift of foresight that I
might engage in careful
planning.

For the gift of wisdom that I
might make sound decisions
and trust in them.

CLOSING: God of wisdom, to
teach with prudence I need
your guidance. For this I
pray. Amen.

ABOUT THE AUTHOR

Sister Gail Mayotte serves as Faculty of Supervision and Instruction for the Alliance for Catholic Education Program at the University of Notre Dame. She is a former teacher, principal, and diocesan curriculum and testing director. Sister Gail is a member of the Congregation of the Sisters of the Assumption of the Blessed Virgin.

The Alliance for Catholic Education Press
at the University of Notre Dame

The Alliance for Catholic Education Press at the University of Notre Dame has established three peer-reviewed publication divisions as part of its effort to support and strengthen the field of Catholic Education. The goal of the press is to publish and disseminate scholarship and educational and spiritual texts and resources in support of the mission of the Alliance for Catholic Education (ACE; **http://ace.nd.edu**). The press publishes books and resources through three divisions.

The Catholic Education Studies division publishes academic and educational writings that promote inquiry and research in Catholic educational traditions, enrich the knowledge base in the field of Catholic education, and foster a broader public understanding of the contributions of Catholic education to the common good. The section publishes books and monographs within and across traditional disciplines in singularly-topical and multi-authored and edited works. Proposals for this section may feature, but are not limited to, inquiry and research on historical, sociological, political, and theological traditions in education, practices, and policy with the potential to impact future stewards, leaders, and scholars in Catholic education.

The Course and Practice-Based Texts and Resources division publishes products for instructional purposes in K-12 schools and university programs of teacher and leadership preparation. Candidate texts and resources should have a well-defined target audience, a focused topic of interest to students, teachers, administrators, and/or teacher educators, and support Catholic education. Products may range from course textbooks and curriculum to supplemental readings and activities guides.

The Spiritual and Pastoral Texts and Resources division publishes products that nourish the spiritual and pastoral needs of students, teachers, and administrators in K-12 Catholic education. These may include prayer and reflective readings, retreat resources, and inspirational texts for children and adults. Potential authors are encouraged to think creatively within the expansive Catholic spiritual tradition to include the many forms of prayer and cultures that enrich this tradition. Proposals should identify the specific target audience and settings for the text or resource.

To learn more about the Alliance for Catholic Education Press at the University of Notre Dame, visit us on the web at **http://www.nd.edu/~acepress**. E-mail inquiries should be sent to **acepress@nd.edu**. To learn more about the Alliance for Catholic Education, visit **http://ace.nd.edu**.

Beyond Alternative Teacher Education:
Integrating Teaching, Community, Spirituality and
Leadership

Edited by John L. Watzke

In Beyond Alternative Teacher Education, John Watzke and his fellow contributors present a bold vision for teacher education that moves the dialogue into new realms of inquiry. Pairing teacher reflective narratives with scholarly chapters, the volume presents the case for programs of teacher formation based in the communal, social and spiritual dimensions of teaching and educational leadership. Beginning with historical tradition and program design, the book also speaks to the importance of the work of program graduates, their professional preparedness, and leadership development. Beyond Alternative Teacher Education will challenge readers to reexamine their notions of what it means to be prepared for work in education and to serve society through education.

"Beyond Alternative Teacher Education presents the case for ACE as the continuing of a tradition of 'service and justice' as carried out by the educational ministry of religious orders. The three 'pillars' of ACE, i.e., professional development, community and spirituality, show that ACE is more than simply an alternative teacher preparation program, it is a model of faith in action and a model of teacher formation."
Thomas C. Hunt, Professor of Education, University of Dayton,
Co-editor, Catholic Education: A Journal of Inquiry & Practice

"Community, spirituality and leadership-these are not themes sounded frequently in discussions of teacher education. Beyond Alternative Teacher Education, however, puts them at the center, thereby creating a collection that offers new perspectives on what 'alternative' teacher education might mean. This is a book for all teacher educators."
Anne Ruggles Gere, Professor of English and Professor of Education,
University of Michigan Past President, National Council of Teachers of English

"Beyond Alternative Teacher Education makes an important and unique contribution to the field of teacher education. It moves this dialogue past the short-sighted political fray and into enduring, real and compelling issues of teacher formation. The volume's chapters effectively pair scholarship and practical experience. The ACE programmatic model, one that merges professional, communal, and spiritual traditions in Catholic education, has grown nationally as a movement in programs of teacher and leadership education. This work represents a foundational and significant contribution to the field of Catholic education and the study of teacher formation."
Terry A. Osborn
Professor and Chair, Division of Curriculum and Teaching, Fordham University